T0041541

WHO ATE WHAT?

A Historical Guessing Game for Food Lovers

BY RACHEL LEVIN

ILLUSTRATED BY NATALIA ROJAS CASTRO

For Hazel and Oren, who ate a lot of avocado rolls
just last night.—RL

For Marge, my favorite chef in the world.—NRC

Phaidon Press Inc.
65 Bleecker Street
New York, NY 10012

phaidon.com

First published 2023
© 2023 Phaidon Press Limited
Text © 2023 Rachel Levin
Illustrations © 2023 Natalia Rojas Castro

Artwork created digitally

ISBN 978 1 83866 690 3 (US edition)
006-0123

A CIP catalog record for this book is available from the
Library of Congress.

All rights reserved. No part of this publication may be
reproduced, stored in a retrieval system or transmitted, in any
form or by any means, electronic, mechanical, photocopying,
recording or otherwise, without the written permission of
Phaidon Press Limited.

The recipes in this book are designed for children but assume
adult supervision at all times. It is up to parents and caregivers
to choose appropriate recipes and ingredients and ensure the
safety of the children under their supervision.

Commissioning Editor: Maya Gartner
Project Editor: Alice-May Bermingham
Production Controller: Rebecca Price
Design: Ana Teodoro, Cantina

Printed in China

What is one thing you do that cavepeople did,
ancient Egyptians did, and astronauts do every day?

The answer is EAT! But do you know what ninjas ate?
And did pirates really eat leather?
Who ate what, and why, depends on **who** they were,
and **where** and **when** they lived.

Turn the page to travel back in time and
journey around the world to guess who ate what!

What did CAVEPEOPLE eat?

Welcome to the Stone Age! Earth's early modern humans, also called Paleolithic people, evolved at least 200,000 years ago. They lived—and ate!—all over the world, and very differently from how we live—and eat—today. There weren't any restaurants or supermarkets. People had to hunt and gather food wherever they could find it. What delicious (and not so delicious) things do you think cavepeople ate? Look at the food in the scene and take a guess!

MILK

OLIVES

WATER CHESTNUTS

FISH

CATTAILS

FIGS

MAMMOTH

ACORNS

WILD
BERRIES

PIZZA

STONES

THISTLE
SEEDS

DATES

BONES

ANTELOPE

WILD CABBAGE

CAVEPEOPLE
ate acorns!

And whatever else they could get their hands on! They gathered and hunted food local to where they lived. This may have included nuts, seeds, and even weeds. Food has evolved over time—and likely looked a little different then. (Picture potatoes the size of peanuts!) And, once fire was discovered, they roasted all kinds of meat and fish. What about dessert? Well, cake and cookies didn't exist back then. . . Guess what they ate instead? Wild fruit! Tiny bits of date have even been found stuck in the teeth of the remains of a 40,000-year-old early human!

ON THE MENU

ACORNS
Found in the wild and roasted. **Try the recipe at the back of the book!**

CATTAILS
Eaten corn-on-the-cob style, these tall reedy marsh plants were crunchy and slightly sweet.

WILD CABBAGE
Prehistoric veggies and leafy plants were commonly eaten in the late Stone Age.

WATER CHESTNUTS
These crunchy and slightly sweet vegetables (not nuts!) grow in water.

THISTLE SEEDS
Thistle is a fast-growing weed, full of nutrients for busy cavepeople.

OLIVES
Tiny fruit (yes, fruit!) that is very bitter when picked straight from the tree.

DATES
Chewy fruit that grows on date palm trees. Nature's candy!

FIGS
Soft, sweet pink fruit filled with little seeds. Possibly similar to today's figs.

BONES
Cavepeople would have sucked out gooey marrow from inside the bone.

WILD BERRIES
Smaller than the ones you eat today, but still a tasty snack.

FISH
Caught using wooden spears and probably cooked over an open fire.

ANTELOPE AND MAMMOTH
Some of the oldest cave art ever found was of people hunting these with bows and arrows.

OFF THE MENU

PIZZA
Cheese, bread, and tomato sauce didn't exist yet. And neither did pizza delivery!

MILK
Early humans couldn't digest animal milk, so it would have made them sick.

STONES
Eons ago, dinosaurs may have eaten rocks to help digest food, but people did not!

What did ANCIENT EGYPTIANS eat?

Building all those massive pyramids must have required a lot of energy! Over their 3,000-year existence as a civilization, Ancient Egyptians ate all sorts of things. We know some of the foods they ate 4,500 years ago because mummified meats have been found in very, very old tombs. They often buried meat like toad or mutton, as it was believed the dead needed to be fed. People enjoyed fresh fruits such as pomegranates, and grains such as barley were used to make pastries, bread, and beer. What do you think pharaohs and other Egyptians ate?

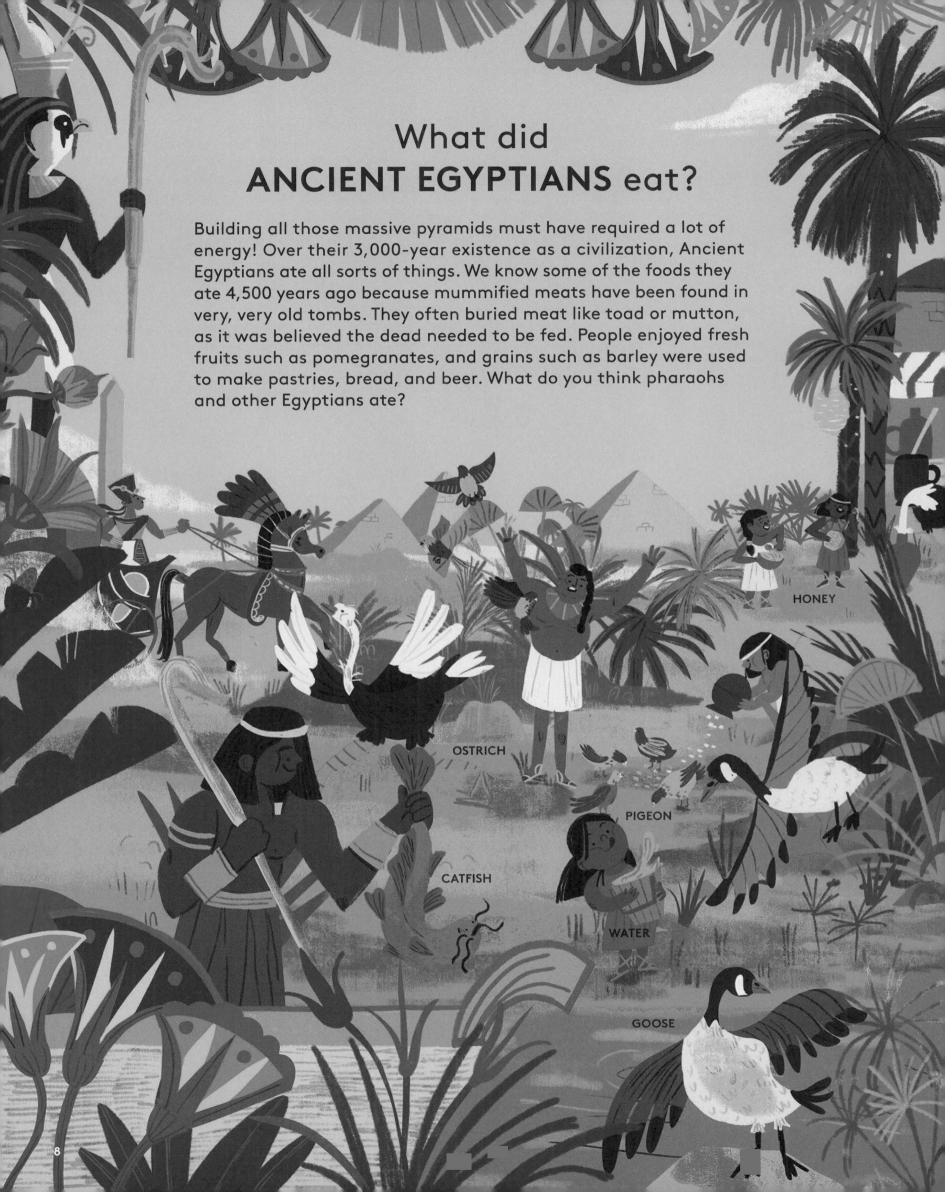

HONEY

OSTRICH

PIGEON

CATFISH

WATER

GOOSE

BEER

GOAT

BREAD

TIGER NUTS

HIPPO

PERCH

HEDGEHOG

POMEGRANATES

MOUSE

ANCIENT EGYPTIANS
ate hippos!

And lots more. The Nile River, one of the longest rivers in the world, runs through Egypt, and all that water provided healthy soil for growing crops. Ancient Egyptians looked after many different animals, some of which were not just a source of food, but symbolic, too. Pharaohs and other wealthy people enjoyed a wide variety of food, from honey-soaked pastries to spiced and roasted meats. They also sat at tables and often had servants bring them food. Poorer people had to sit on mats on the floor. All people ate with their fingers, though—even pharaohs!

ON THE MENU

HIPPOS
Hunting hippopotami was a dangerous task, and a sign of courage and strength.

POMEGRANATES
A symbol of health and prosperity, these were also used to make wine.

HONEY
A luxury. 3,000-year-old honey has even been found in Egyptian tombs!

TIGER NUTS
Not nuts but tubers that were ground into flour to make cakes. **Try the recipe at the back of the book!**

BREAD
Made from grains, like emmer, that were ground into flour and baked in various shapes and sizes.

BEER
Brewing water with barley killed germs and made weak beer.

CATFISH
A symbol of dominance, served boiled or roasted.

GOOSE
Their meat and livers were roasted over hot embers.

PIGEON
Served roasted and stuffed. It's still enjoyed as a delicacy in Egypt today.

OSTRICH
Eaten as meat. Their big eggs were supposedly hollowed into dishes.

GOAT
Meats such as honey-roasted goat were enjoyed by rich Egyptians.

HEDGEHOG
Baked in clay. When the clay was removed, their spines came off with it.

OFF THE MENU

PERCH
In some places people considered this fish too sacred to eat, as were otters, eels, and some other creatures.

MOUSE
Not eaten as food, but holding a warm dead mouse in your mouth was thought to cure a toothache!

WATER
Nope—water from the Nile was dirty and made people sick, so everyone drank weak beer.

What did the AZTECS eat?

We owe so much to the Aztecs, including some of our favorite foods! Hardworking, inventive agricultural people, the Aztecs lived from the 1200s to the 1500s in Mesoamerica, an area covering southern North America and most of Central America. Crops were grown on chinampas, which were like floating gardens on shallow lake beds. So what food did the Aztecs grow?

COWS

POPCORN

MAIZE

SUGAR

NOPAL CACTUS

GRASSHOPPERS AND ANTS

MUSCOVY DUCKS

SPIRULINA

HOT CHOCOLATE

IGUANA

AVOCADO

BEANS

DOG

CHEESY
QUESADILLAS

TOMATOES

13

AZTECS
ate cacti!

And lots of maize and corn, which were used to make almost everything they ate, including oatmeal, tortillas, and tamales. Favorite dishes included roasted iguana, salamander, and armadillo! They had festive midnight feasts, where they would throw food on the ground as a gift to the gods. The Aztecs were among the first to discover chocolate, and made a chili-spiced hot chocolate drink known as xocoatl. It was so good that one emperor, called Moctezuma, supposedly drank 50 cups a day!

ON THE MENU

NOPAL CACTUS
Also called "prickly pear."
Can you see why?
Aztecs believed it helped
cure many illnesses.

GRASSHOPPERS AND ANTS
These crunchy critters taste
earthy and nutty. As for ants:
some say lemony!

TOMATOES
Red, green, and gold
varieties were grown. Aztecs
may have been the first
people to eat tomatoes.

MAIZE
For nearly everything!
It was thought to be a gift
from the god Quetzalcoatl.

AVOCADO
Spanish conquistadors
called mashed avocado
(guacamole) "poor
man's butter."

DOG
Small dogs were more
likely to be raised for dinner
than kept as pets.

MUSCOVY DUCKS
Not just dinner! Their
feathers were used to make
coats for the Aztec rulers.

BEANS
Soaked in water then boiled
until soft, and often spiced
and served at every meal.

POPCORN
Popped corn kernels weren't
just eaten. They were also
strung into necklaces
and used on headdresses.

SPIRULINA
Blue-green lake algae was
sun-dried and made into
high-energy cake squares.

XOCOATL
(HOT CHOCOLATE)
A drink considered worthy
of the gods. **Try the recipe
at the back of the book!**

IGUANA
Nicknamed "chicken of the
trees" because—that's right
—it tastes like chicken!

OFF THE MENU

BEEF (COW)
Didn't arrive in the Americas until the
late 1400s or early 1500s, around when
the Aztec Empire was ending.

CHEESY QUESADILLAS
No cows, sheep, or goats
meant no cheese,
which meant no quesadillas!

SUGAR
Aztecs didn't have sugar, so they used
other natural sweeteners such as honey,
cinnamon, vanilla, and fruit.

What did VIKINGS eat?

The Vikings are often referred to as raiders, but they were also traders and warriors, craftspeople and farmers. They lived from the 8th to 11th centuries, in what's now Scandinavia. Eventually, they traveled to the UK, Greenland, Iceland, and even as far as North America. We don't know exactly what the Vikings ate, but we do know they ate a lot. And lots of different things. But not everything. . . Guess what they did, and did not, eat!

BEAR

REINDEER

ELK

PIG

OXEN

SKYR

MUSHROOMS

PEACHES

BERRIES

OATMEAL

ORANGE CARROTS

BREAD

STEWS

HERRING

FRESH CHEESE

FISH FROM THE SEA

VIKINGS
ate herring!

And not many fresh fruits or vegetables. Growing crops year-round wasn't possible due to the colder seasons where Vikings lived, so they salted, smoked, or fermented food in barrels of whey (the watery part of milk) to help the food last longer. It was the Viking version of a refrigerator. They ate lots of meat and lots of gruel, a thin oatmeal. Boiling was popular, as was grilling and roasting over a fire, with giant frying pans and large iron pots. Meals were served in wooden bowls, with spoons made of wood or even bone! Vikings hunted and ate using sharp dagger knives, fishing meat out of shared pots using giant pronged forks.

ON THE MENU

HERRING
Vikings preserved fish and other foods over winter by drying, smoking, pickling, or salting them.

OATMEAL
Breakfast gruel made from barley and oats, sometimes topped with berries.

SKYR
A thick yogurt made from cow's milk that is still enjoyed around the world.

BERRIES
Tart wild cloudberries, lingonberries, and strawberries.

FRESH CHEESE
Made by hand from the milk of goats, sheep, and cows.

BEAR
Only the bravest and most elite hunters would dare hunt a bear.

ELK AND REINDEER
Plentiful and high in protein, reindeer were used for their milk, too.

OXEN
Used for both hauling machinery on farms and for food.

PORK (PIG)
According to Viking myth, honored warriors ate pork in Valhalla (Viking heaven).

STEWS
These were probably made with whatever meat they had available.

MUSHROOMS
Vikings ate many kinds of these from the forest, just not the poisonous ones!

BREAD
In all shapes and sizes—round, rectangular, flat, even doughnut-shaped!

OFF THE MENU

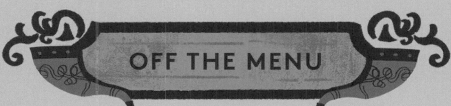

ORANGE CARROTS
Not orange ones! Carrots were white and purple in Viking times.

FISH FROM THE SEA
Even though Vikings traveled by sea a lot, they didn't fish on the go. They mainly fished in rivers and streams.

PEACHES
It was far too cold to grow peaches.

What did MEDIEVAL MONARCHS eat?

It was a time of castles and kings, lords and ladies, and serfs and peasants. Europe's medieval period lasted from the 500s to the 1500s. Monarchs and very wealthy people had cooks to make their food. Peasants cooked for themselves—mostly cabbage and stews. For royalty, meals were an event. They ate all sorts of things—on special occasions, at least. Can you guess what?

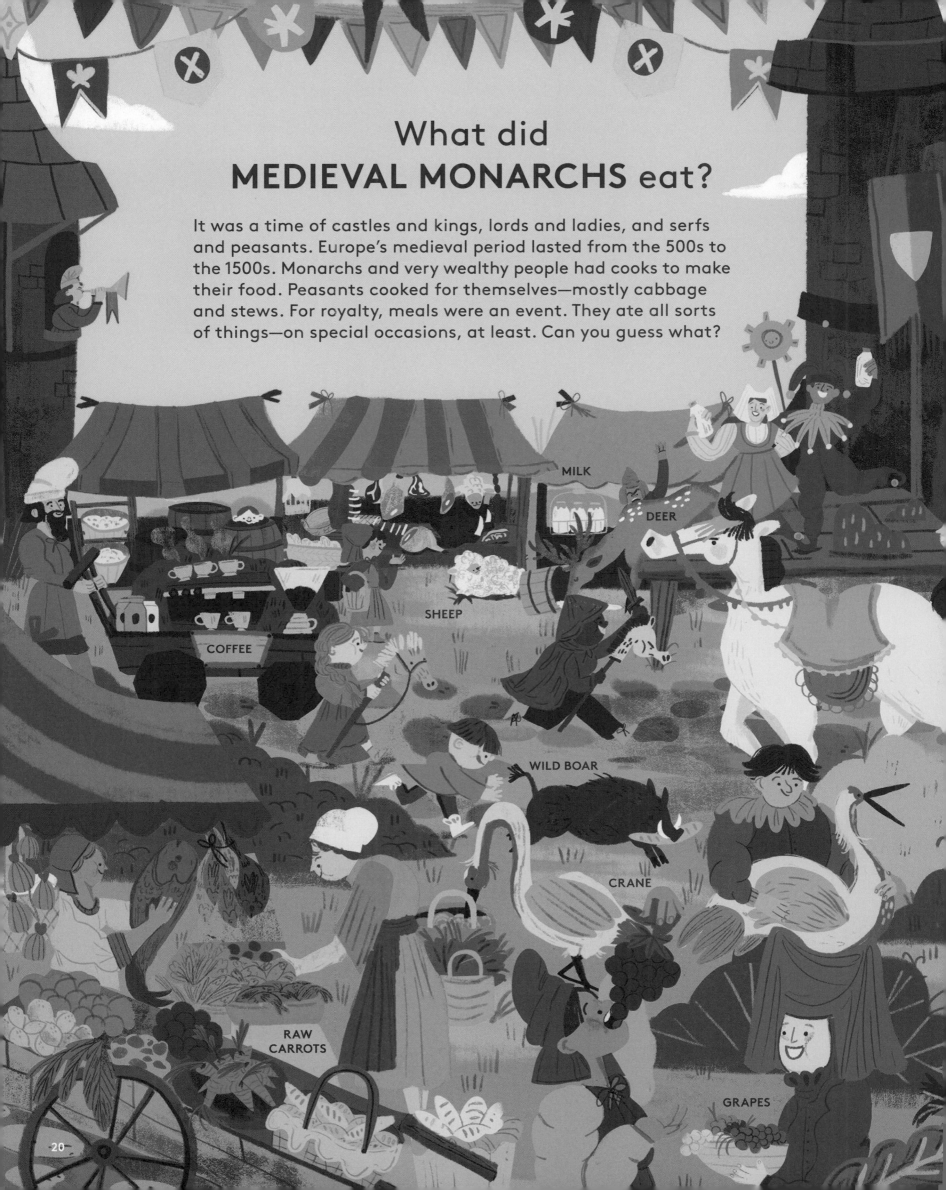

MILK

DEER

SHEEP

COFFEE

WILD BOAR

CRANE

RAW CARROTS

GRAPES

WHALE

PIE

HERRING
AND SALMON

SWAN

BREAD

PEACOCK

OYSTERS

PEAS

MEDIEVAL MONARCHS
ate mutton!

And much, much more. Dinner was a big deal for medieval kings and queens. Each night, they might be showered with 10-course meals! Bowls of water were set out for handwashing as they cut food with sharp daggers and then ate with their fingers. Food was washed down with lots of beer, cider, or wine. Dinner was often announced by horn, with jesters, jugglers, and musicians. Manners were important. No elbows on the table, no burping, no farting, and definitely no picking noses!

ON THE MENU

MUTTON (SHEEP)
Popular with the wealthy!
They would spit-roast an
entire sheep over a fire.

WILD BOAR
Hunted in kings' private
forests, wild boar was
a prized dinner.

BREAD
Darker and denser than
today's and sometimes
used as a plate!

VENISON (DEER)
Lean meat from hunted
deer was "seethed" (boiled)
in a giant cauldron.

WHALE
Considered a "royal fish,"
its meat, blubber, and even
tongues were eaten.

PEAS
Cooked fresh, not from
frozen! These were a popular
medieval vegetable.

SWAN AND PEACOCK
Roasted whole with their
feathers on to make
an impressive centerpiece.

HERRING AND SALMON
Fish was served fresh,
salted, or smoked
depending on the season.

GRAPES
Turned into wine all across
southern Europe.

OYSTERS
A briny, meaty treat for
those near the coast.

CRANE
Anything with wings
was popular to eat.

PIE
Mutton pies, pork pies,
prune-and-parsley pies. . .
People loved all kinds of pies!

OFF THE MENU

RAW CARROTS
It was believed that raw produce caused
disease, so veggies, like carrots,
were battered into "fried skirwittes."

COFFEE
Neither coffee nor tea had
arrived in Europe, so beer or
apple cider was drunk instead.

MILK
Sometimes given to children, but
animal milk didn't stay fresh for long.
Commoners drank apple and pear cider.

What did NINJAS eat?

Ninjas were tiny but mighty! Also known as shinobi, they were Japanese spies who may have been around as early as the 12th century. They were able to scurry up trees and scale walls, swing from ropes and hang from rafters. They were sneaky and always on the go, which means their food needed to provide lots of energy and be easy to carry. So what snacks did ninjas often have with them?

SNAKE

GREEN TEA ICE CREAM

RICE

FROG

RED MEAT

GARLIC

THIRST BALLS

PINE NUTS

SALTED FISH

TOFU

CHINESE
YAMS

HUNGER
BALLS

QUAIL EGGS

BLACK
SESAME SEEDS

GRASSHOPPERS

NINJAS
ate snakes!

And foods without strong odors, because a smelly ninja was a dead ninja! After all, a ninja's whole job was to spy on their enemies. Always on the move, they carried sacks of "hunger balls," packed with carrots and licorice root. They kept ninjas well fueled, and were a bit like the energy bars we have today. They also packed "thirst balls", made with mashed pickled plums and other good stuff. They were like edible water bottles! Some food was used as secret codes between ninjas, such as salted fish, which supposedly meant "beware of danger."

ON THE MENU

SNAKE
Supposedly some ninjas captured and ate snakes. Consider it spies' spaghetti!

GRASSHOPPERS
Tiny, nutritious, one-bite snacks that spies could pop into their mouths like popcorn.

FROG
These jumpy amphibians were abundant and nutritious.

SALTED FISH
Easy nutritious snacking. It is thought they were used to send secret messages.

TOFU
Healthy and mild in flavor and scent, this was the perfect food for a ninja.

PINE NUTS
Seeds were thought to help keep ninjas' five senses young and alert.

QUAIL EGGS
Ninjas believed eating these helped them hide.

BLACK SESAME SEEDS
Black-colored foods were believed to help keep ninjas warm and active.

RICE
Often mixed with rice wine or hot water to keep ninjas warm in winter.

THIRST BALLS
Made with mashed pickled plums, rye ergot fungus, and sugar.

CHINESE YAMS
Found in hunger balls and packed full of starchy energy.

HUNGER BALLS
Pocket-sized nutritious rice balls—perfect for secret missions.

OFF THE MENU

RED MEAT
This was believed to dull their senses. Ninjas needed to stay sharp!

GARLIC
Way too smelly! If ninjas ate this, their breath would surely blow their cover!

GREEN TEA ICE CREAM
No ice cream yet. (Can you imagine a world without ice cream?!)

What did PIRATES eat?

As early as the 1500s, pirate ships would set sail for months at a time, with no land in sight—apart from perhaps the occasional deserted island. From the Caribbean Sea to the Atlantic and Indian Oceans, pirates everywhere were explorers and adventurers, often rebels and plunderers. Out at sea, without refrigerators, gardens, or markets, what could pirates possibly have eaten?

BUTTER

HARDTACK

FISH

CHOCOLATE COINS

LOCUSTS

COW

CHEESE

ARMADILLO

LEATHER
SATCHELS

EGGS

CHICKEN

RUM

FLAMINGO

ORANGES
AND LEMONS

HUMAN
EYES

PIRATES
ate eggs!

And anything else fresh first, while it lasted. At the beginning of a journey, the ship might be stocked with fresh food. But as the months wore on, everyone would have to make do with what they had. Which wasn't much. Or all that tasty. Before long, it would all be gone or spoil—with only a hardened biscuit called hardtack left. Lots of stale-tasting, tooth-chipping, not-so-delicious hardtack. . .

ON THE MENU

EGGS
For as long as the chickens lasted. . .

CHEESE
Hard local cheese was a treat, until it ran out. . .

BUTTER
Stored in barrels and used for cooking and flavor.

CHICKEN
Chickens that had stopped laying eggs were dinner!

FLAMINGO
"Very good meat," wrote famous pirate William Dampier in his journal.

BEEF (COW)
Dried and salted in barrels. The beef was so tough, some carved it into belts!

ARMADILLO
Dampier also reported it "tastes much like land-turtle."

LOCUSTS
"Very moist, their heads would crackle in one's teeth," Dampier added.

HARDTACK
Sturdy squares of cooked flour, salt, and water. **Try the recipe at the back of the book!**

RUM
Water stored in barrels turned green and slimy, so after weeks at sea, pirates had to drink rum.

ORANGES AND LEMONS
Eaten to ward off an illness called scurvy, which is caused by lack of vitamin C.

LEATHER SATCHELS
A stranded ship ran out of food, so pirates shredded and fried their satchels!

OFF THE MENU

FISH
Pirates didn't actually eat all that much fish—the ship had to keep moving, and catching fish took time.

CHOCOLATE COINS
For a hungry pirate, these would have been worth more than real gold, but milk chocolate didn't even exist yet.

HUMAN EYES
Some say pirates wore a patch to help their eyes better adjust to the dark, not just because they had lost an eye.

What did QING EMPERORS eat?

Eating, for emperors of the Qing dynasty, who ruled China from 1644 to 1912, was seen as a way to maintain or improve a person's health. And it worked! Emperor Qianlong lived to the age of 87, which was a true feat in the 1700s, when people often died in their 50s or 60s. What foods pictured here sound healthy enough to make a meal fit for a king?

DUCK

MOUNTAIN PEARS
AND TANGERINES

SPINACH

PIG

PURPLE
RICE

PEACHES

QING EMPERORS
ate purple rice!

And many other delicacies. Emperors ate two formal meals a day—often sitting at a table alone. Plus snacks! The emperor's first bite could be as early as 4:00 a.m. Lunch was the big meal of the day, and it was a feast fit for one—with anywhere from 7 to 100 dishes! A servant would often first taste each dish to make sure the food wasn't poisoned. An emperor always ate in harmony, balancing the five flavors: sweet, bitter, sour, salty, and spicy.

PURPLE RICE
This nutritious rice was also known as forbidden rice because it was reserved for the wealthy.

BIRD'S NEST
A nest made of solidified bird saliva! Boiled with ginger and broth and made into a soup.

SHARK FIN SOUP
Once a popular dish for the wealthy, today shark fin soup is banned in many places to protect sharks.

PORK LEG (PIG)
Served with seven delicacies: bird's nest, duck, smoked meats, cabbage, chicken wings, pig stomach, and mushrooms.

PEACHES
Stuffed with roasted duck meat.

SPINACH
Stir-fried with small dried shrimp, or stewed.

TOFU
Soybean milk curds pressed into blocks and served with mushrooms.

DUCK
Stewed with wine and cauliflower.

VENISON (DEER)
Deer were hunted, even by emperors, and roasted or steamed.

MOUNTAIN PEARS AND TANGERINES
Fresh and dried fruits were part of the emperor's diet.

TEA
Qing emperors drank tea daily from fancy porcelain sets, often with friends.

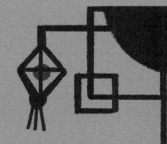

STEAMED BUNS
Stuffed with all sorts of food from pumpkin and mutton to Chinese yam.

OFF THE MENU

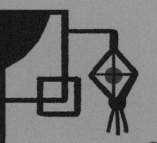

CROW
The emperors considered them sacred, so instead of killing them, people fed and protected them.

FORTUNE COOKIES
Fortune cookies are believed to have originated in Japan. They were popularized by America, at Chinese American restaurants.

BEEF (COW)
The palace considered it a sin to eat a cow, as it was a "beast of burden."

What did ETHIOPIAN EMPRESS TAYTU eat?

In 1887, Empress Taytu, the wife of Emperor Menelik of Ethiopia, threw an enormous five-day feast at her palace overlooking the new capital city of Addis Ababa. She understood that food and politics were connected and knew the feast could help unify people to be part of an emerging country, like Ethiopia. Thousands of Ethiopians came to the feast. What did she serve to all of those people?

CHICKEN STEW

PIG

INJERA

BUTTER

COW

OXEN

SHEEP

SPICES

HONEY
WINE

GINGER

EGGS

LENTILS

COLLARD GREENS

FRESH FRUIT
SALAD

CHICKEN

FRAPPÉ

EMPRESS TAYTU
ate injera!

And lots of other people did too as Empress Taytu hosted a feast with dishes from many different local cultures in one giant tent. Members of the church, servants, nobles, and everyday citizens ate at long wooden tables—though not all at the same time. At 9:00 a.m. each day, the palace guards were fed first so they could then control the crowds jostling to get in. In the evening, the tent was lit by candles and torchlight. Taytu's party formed the beginnings of modern Ethiopian cuisine.

ON THE MENU

INJERA
500 baskets were served of this spongy delicious Ethiopian bread, made with a tiny grain called teff.

HONEY WINE
About 45 jugs of this sweet treat were drunk, as well as barley beer from cow horn cups.

SPICES
Berbere, cinnamon, chilies, salt, and other spices were all used to flavor food.

CHICKEN
Doro dabo, a bread stuffed with chicken, was a favorite of Empress Taytu's.

LENTILS
Misir wot, a spicy lentil stew, was eaten with injera bread.

BEEF (COW)
Kai wot was a beef stew spiced with berbere.

BUTTER
Stored in clay jars to keep it fresh.

OXEN
Cooked into a hearty stew.

GINGER
Used in Emmes, a dish of sautéed meat with spices and butter.

COLLARD GREENS
Hot and healthy dark leafy greens!

CHICKEN AND EGG STEW
Doro wat chicken stew with egg in a crimson-colored butter pepper sauce.

MUTTON (SHEEP)
A hearty dish of mutton ribs in turmeric-spiced broth.

OFF THE MENU

FRESH FRUIT SALAD
Other than bananas and lemons, not much fruit grew in the Ethiopian highlands.

PORK (PIG)
Often not eaten for religious reasons.

FRAPPÉ
No popular and pricey global chain of coffee shops in the 1800s, but lots of black coffee!

What do ASTRONAUTS eat?

Space food has come a long way since 1969, when Neil Armstrong first walked on the moon. Today, astronauts have a huge variety of food. Breakfast, lunch, and dinner in space have to be healthy and last for months, and—most important—not float away while the astronauts are eating it! So what is on the menu in outer space today? And how is it made?

SHRIMP

FISH

KALE

LOBSTER

PIZZA

CHIPS

SODA

COFFEE

POWDERED
DOUGHNUTS

TORTILLA
WRAPS

CARROTS

MACARONI
AND CHEESE

BEEF

CHOCOLATE
PUDDING

TACOS

ASTRONAUTS eat macaroni and cheese!

And lots of other delicious things you might eat, too. In the early days of space travel, astronauts ate apple sauce and puréed beef squeezed from tubes, like toothpaste! Today the food is much tastier. A menu might even be designed by a fancy French chef. Most meals come in vacuum-sealed pouches, where air has been sucked out. Some are ready to eat; others need water or heating. Astronauts use extra-long spoons to reach the bottom of the pouch. The spoons are magnetic so they stick to the tray. Space dulls your taste buds, so dishes have to be extra flavorful. If you ate space food on Earth, it would taste way too salty!

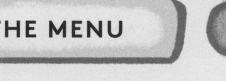

ON THE MENU

MACARONI AND CHEESE
Pasta with cheese sauce. Like at home, only freeze-dried (just add hot water).

CARROT CLAFOUTIS
A baked carrot dish spiced with smoked paprika for extra kick.

KALE SALAD
Veggies are fairly new to space fare. They are soaked in hot water to stay crunchy.

BEEF (COW)
Canned beef with mushroom sauce made to be too thick to float away.

SHRIMP COCKTAIL
Cooked, cold shrimp are served in a pouch with a spicy pink sauce.

TACOS
Featuring fresh chilies harvested from the space station's first crops!

LOBSTER
Cooked longer and hotter than on Earth, and served with lemon sauce.

INDIAN FISH CURRY
When rehydrated (water is added), the curry spice mix gives it flavor.

PIZZA
There's no delivery service in space, so astronauts have DIY pizza parties.

COFFEE
Powdered and served in a pouch with a straw.

TORTILLA WRAPS
Sticky ingredients like peanut butter and honey are best. Plus no bread crumbs with a tortilla!

CHOCOLATE PUDDING
No longer freeze-dried—squeezed straight out of a packet and onto a spoon so it doesn't spill.

OFF THE MENU

CHIPS
Way too many crumbs! They can float into eyes and equipment and cause problems.

FIZZY DRINKS
The bubbles in these would give astronauts tummy troubles if they drank them in space.

POWDERED DOUGHNUTS
Nope. Too messy! A sticky glazed doughnut, however, may be possible. . .

What are WE going to eat in the future?

We can't know for certain what we'll be eating in the next 20 years, let alone the next 200, but we can wonder. Our planet is amazing, and if we treat it right, it will have all the food and water we need to survive. The thing is: our planet also has almost 8 billion people. And it will have millions, even billions, more people to feed in the future. What are some ways we can protect our planet and eat sustainably?

Eat *all* kinds of fish in the sea

People all over the world love eating fish. But we eat too many of the *same* kind of fish (like salmon and tuna), which leads to overfishing. "Blue food" is the wave of the future, but humans will have to expand their fishy taste bud to different kinds of seafood. Lean, protein-packed, and prolific breeders, jellyfish are one of the ocean's most sustainable creatures. You know what else is edible, delicious, and underwater? Seaweed!

Eat insects

Crickets, caterpillars, grasshoppers and, even earthworms. In many places around the world, people already eat insects. Filled with vitamins, and of course found *everywhere,* insects are really good for you *and* the environment. Someday, we may be eating ant cereal, cockroach milk, silkworm ice cream, or even cricket chips!

Whatever we eat in the decades to come, it is sure to be exciting. And hopefully delicious.

What do **YOU** think you might be eating in the future?

Eat more plants and less meat

Large cattle ranches are not good for climate change. Cows burp! And emit greenhouse gasses that contribute to global warming. The more plants, and less meat, people eat, the better! The Aztecs understood the power of plants: they ate loads of nopal cactus, or prickly pear, for health and nutrients, and it's still eaten in salads and tacos. There are hundreds of kinds of edible cacti in the world, and they all require a lot less water than cows!

Invent new forms of meat

Plant-based meat is very popular. And soon enough, meat and fish—like chicken nuggets, fish sticks, and steak—will come from laboratories. Scientists have been working hard to create meat in a science lab, grown from the cells of animals. You know what a lab-based chicken nugget looks—and tastes—like? Like a chicken nugget!

We may not be able to travel back in time, but we can try. . . by sampling some tasty (or not-so-tasty?) historical snacks.

Eat like a CAVEPERSON

Do you remember, from the beginning of this book, one little tiny thing early humans likely loved to eat? Acorns! Don't eat them raw though, and ask an adult for help with the cooking.

Roasted Acorns

Ingredients:

Acorns, as many as you want to eat
Salt to taste (even if cavepeople couldn't!)

You can buy acorns in bulk, but it's more fun to gather them like a caveperson. They fall from oak trees. Look for smooth brown ones with their caps still on. Only collect freshly fallen acorns. Shell and remove the caps. Spread them out on a hard surface and smash with a rolling pin. Soak in warm water for a few hours, then rinse. Boil the raw shell-less acorns until the water turns dark brown. Strain. Boil again until it the water is clear. Strain, let dry. Preheat the oven to 320°F. Scatter on a baking sheet and roast for an hour, occasionally rolling them around. Roast until they turn brown and start to smell like, well, roasted nuts. Salt and eat!

Eat like an ANCIENT EGYPTIAN

The Ancient Egyptians left behind mummified foods, which helped food historians figure out what they ate— and to come up with this recipe for a sweet cakey treat.

Tiger Nut Honey Cake

Ingredients:

1 ½ cups tiger nut flour
1 ½ cups whole wheat flour
⅓ cup whole milk
2 eggs
3 tablespoons melted butter, plus more for frying
½ cup honey

Combine ingredients, then knead into a dough. On a lightly floured surface, roll the dough out into a rectangle, 0.5 in thick. Cut into four squares, then cut the squares diagonally to create small triangles. Melt about 2 tablespoons of butter in a frying pan over medium heat. Place as many triangles of dough as you can fit into the pan and fry on one side for 2 minutes. Then flip them, drizzle honey into the pan, and fry on the other side for 2 minutes. Repeat with the rest, and serve warm.

Ask an adult to smash, simmer, or bake with you.

Eat like a PIRATE

True to its name, hardtack is. . . hard. Simple to make, hardtack was a pirate's most popular snack at sea. Spread it with peanut butter or jelly, or just eat it like the pirates used to: plain.

Hardtack

Ingredients:

2 cups flour
½ tablespoon salt
½ to ¾ cup water

Preheat oven to 350°F. Combine flour with salt in a mixing bowl. Add water and mix with your hands until the dough comes together. Roll out on a table to about 0.5 in thick. Use a knife to cut small squares from the dough. Place on a baking sheet and use a chopstick to make 16 evenly spaced holes in each square. Bake for at least four hours, turning over once halfway through baking. Cool on a rack in a dry room.

Drink like an AZTEC

The Aztecs made all kinds of chocolate drinks: honeyed chocolate, red chocolate (to resemble blood!), and a bitter chocolate drink called xocoatl. Xocoatl was made with chili, so it was spicy.

Xocoatl, Hot Chocolate

Ingredients:

4 cups of milk or water
2 cups of unsweetened Mexican chocolate chunks
1 cinnamon stick
1 chili pepper, split and seeded
1 teaspoon vanilla extract

In a saucepan, simmer the milk over medium heat. Stir in the Mexican chocolate and simmer. Add the cinnamon stick and vanilla, and stir. (Add a chili, too, if you want it spicy!) Remove the cinnamon stick and whisk until frothy. Pour into cups, add a cinnamon stick, and serve. If you want to drink it like the Aztecs, let it cool until it's lukewarm. Drink it hot if you'd rather warm up on a cold day. Emperor Moctezuma drank from a goblet of solid gold. But an ordinary mug will do!

Note from the author

Researching what humans ate eons ago wasn't easy! I relied on the input, and kindness, of many experts, including: Shanghai-based New York University professor Joanna Waley-Cohen; Kate Spence at the University of Cambridge; Peter Ungar at the University of Arkansas; the University of Pittsburg's Harry Kloman; Neil Price at Sweden's Uppsala University; and Ryan Dowdy, ex-NASA food scientist now focused on the future. I also leaned on research from trusted sources like museums and academic articles, respected publications like *National Geographic* and *Atlas Obscura*, organizations like the International Ninja Research Center, nonfiction books, and one of the world's very first cookbooks. Even fun websites, such as Pass the Flamingo, run by Andrew Coletti, who graciously granted us permission for the Tiger Nut Honey Cake recipe, as well as Jacqueline Newman's *Flavor and Fortune*. Given that, in some cases, little to no culinary records were kept (and that most people who lived during many of the periods presented in this book are, well, dead), we can only try to accurately piece together what people throughout time really, truly ate. So please, kids and adults, enjoy this book with a grain of salt.

About the author

Rachel Levin is the author of *Look Big: And Other Tips for Surviving Animal Encounters of All Kinds*, and co-author of the cookbooks *Eat Something* and *Steamed*. She is also a journalist, a mother, and a very good eater in San Francisco. You can find out more about Rachel at byrachellevin.com.

About the illustrator

Natalia Rojas Castro is an illustrator from Bogotá, Colombia. Her illustrations are inspired by the colors and nature of Colombia and the streets of Bogotá, where she lives. Food is very important to her, especially the "ajiaco," a Colombian soup that warms the body on cold Bogotá days, made by her mom, her favorite chef.